Haikus

to Irish

Tunes

Erin Flanagan

Illustrations Copyright © 2023 by Kelly Flanagan
Illustrations Copyright © 2023 by Megan Flanagan
Illustrations Copyright © 2023 by Evan Hansen

Edited by Flor Ana Mireles

1st Edition | 01
Paperback ISBN: 979-8-9862106-2-9
Ebook ISBN: 979-8-9862106-3-6

First Published January 2023

Printed in the USA   1 2 3 4 5 6 7 8 9 10

For inquiries and bulk orders, please email:
indieearthpublishinghouse@gmail.com

Indie Earth Publishing Inc.
| Miami, FL |
www.indieearthbooks.com

INDIE EARTH

Praise for *Haikus to Irish Tunes*

"*Haikus to Irish Tunes* is a unique addition to the haiku world. Flanagan provides a new take at haiku through her humor and crafty use of Irish songs."
— Luke Levi, Author of *So Fragile Are the Beautiful Things*

"Flanagan's words transport us to a music-fulled pub in Ireland, to a park bench enjoying a spring day and beyond. Her haikus create wonderful scenes we need to be a part of. This is a must-have collection of poetry."
— RJ Tungsten, Author of *Girasole - A Walk Through The Seasons*

"Flanagan has awoken a love for haikus that I didn't know I had. *Haikus to Irish Tunes* combines simple, yet intricate three-line poetry that leaves a sweetness for life, nature, and music. Loved this pocketbook of poems."
— Flor Ana, Author of *The Language of Fungi & Flowers*

"Flanagan's haikus flow with a cadence that feels almost musical. I love this book."
— Gabe Henry, Author of *Eating Salad Drunk: Haikus for the Burnout Age by Comedy Greats*

"*Haikus to Irish Tunes* leaves you thinking of more meaning to the depth behind the tunes of the haikus. A pleasant read and insight to what is important to Erin Flanagan."
— Kendall Hope, Author of *Pockets of Lavender*

Praise for *Haikus to Irish Tunes*

"*Haikus to Irish Tunes* is such an enjoyable poetry collection. It was interesting to see different subjects, like spring and listening to music, broken into little pieces. Haiku-writing is a difficult format to maintain, and Erin Flanagan nails it."
— Rachel Finkle, Author of *Raspberry Fingers*

"Short, sweet, and to the point. The page can only hold so much before the soul is touched, and that's how these poems felt to me."
— Mari Pizzini, Starred Review*

Reviews have been edited for clarity and length.

Haikus to Irish Tunes

Erin Flanagan

To pathways that keep us sane
Loved ones who keep us humble
And traditional music that opens its arms to the future

Hearing Things, Danced by Strings

(1)
A primitive Yeaux!
A signature shift tableaux
Ecstasy Released

(2)
The birds tweets sweeter,
Heard faintly o'er the tunes
Than sharp and alone

(3)
Moans plucked, shrill gasps blown.
Whistle soaring on a breeze
Strums pull tense; yet free

(4)
Flying melody
Pipes and whistles, shrill and clear
So she may dance

(5)
Rhythms synthesize
Throws of blues, greens, yellows.
Vivid reality

(6)
Brim-filled excuses
Trilling flight, Free of constraints
Spurred on toward joy

(7)
Eye contact, ladies,
Concerned to have and avoid.
Smile, the tune spoke for you

(8)
A jigs, a jigs a
Jig: Notes peppered in a stride
Free in pendulum

(9)
In worlds of much new,
Old greats lay in dormant base
Fear they burial?

(10)
Hum along da-dum
That rift you vaguely recall—
Qualify spring breath

(11)
The band takes a breath
Returns with a jolt back in
A new signature

(12)
Thump-thump, thump, thump-thump.
For you, seven notes of tune
How they do connect

(13)
Sounds the running stream
"Vivid sonic images"
Napier shall paint me

(14)
Drive by doppler
Mistake those uilleann pipes
Hear that siren's call

(15)
Sean nos, a hunger,
In the fleeting gloaming.
Tweets echo

(16)
An Oriole's song,
The start to the jig you know
You never knew

(17)
Oh, don't nap too long,
The pipes in your ear, a glare,
Infinitely reflecting in a fog

(18)
I took two weeks off
From listening to words sung,
Looking for enough

(19)
Extend out your arms
Tempo is the same, it's just
The anticipation

(20)
A fusion of souls
The jazz flute isn't funny
Please let it move you

(21)
"Please sing again!"
I DM-begged an artist
In obscurity

(22)
Making music
Fingers tapping, a bodhran,
Eyes dancing a reel

(23)
Ornamentation
Is the emotion, not the
Surface aesthetics

(24)
Just keeping time, but
Into this tune I would morph
If the soul had a say

(25)
Clancys formed my thoughts
These tunes are my genetics:
Barely even Irish

(26)
Flute and bodhran switch—
Purpose designated
Bass and melody

(27)
Like the Hawks cry, or
The prehistoric Cypress,
Tunes seem elemental

(28)
The pipe's keen voice
Needs to be exhumed from this
Fairied history

(29)
The pipe's yearning voice
Induces feeling today
Even if nostalgic

(30)
Sean nos holds this heart
To dreams and fantasies
Of current wants

(31)
Riding no-handed
Winds trap tunes in my ears
Bass drummed on chest and thighs

(32)
Can't believe these feet
Haven't danced with real beat
Since 2015

(33)
"Too-ra-loo ra-lai"
Voice, the instrument, does not
Stop in absence of words

(34)
Transcended to space
When tunes catch you off guard
Whole body absorption

(35)
This music begs you
To participate
Your taps play a part

(36)
The snare pops 3/4
Sparkling sound of the show
Attention seeking

(37)
Lord of the Dance plays
Child slathers kisses on screen
For Siamsa dancers

(38)
The music tells of
Awful joys and great sorrows.
Close like chirps and cricks

(39)
Chirps in 8 rays
A symphonic morning
Song

Spring's Pistol

(40)
Four buds bloomed this week,
January's miracle.
You unfollowed me

(41)
Honey hints the air
Too soft, these new white blooms seem
Near thorny locusts

(42)
6 o'clock, suburban spring
An eternity of peace.
Bells toll local now

(43)
Bright against the green
Daffodils and lavender
Sublime minute

(44)
Little Cardinal
Landed on a branch
Swayed from momentum

(45)
You don't think of baby crows
Or caring for the nest
Mama crows

(46)
Coned seeds droop
Sometimes perfectly shaped
You want to pick them

(47)
Infinite blue space
Between green destinations
Black silhouette in flight

(48)
Bluebird drops near,
I glance around,
And might speak softly

(49)
Amusing Robin
Fleet legg'd, trots with dangling worm
'Fore the golden dusk

(50)
Clouds drifted away
Sun buttered the canopy.
Off leaves, rain fell still

(51)
Our myth transposed—
Archetypes insufficient
To gangly saplings

(52)
Catbird shrills maniacally
When spring uniformly blooms.
Doubt: Only sign of sanity

(53)
Rain droplets
Light the tree
In the moonlight

(54)
The red of new growth
A trick to those who have
Never paid attention before

(55)
Sunset after storm
Orange mellows the clouds
Lovely remainder

(56)
Highway driving.
Smog does not distort
Leaves definition

(57)
Mid afternoon highway
Overlooked by spotted clouds
One burst—dusts the road

(58)
The weed's stems bend—Arms
Reaching to rejoice and praise
The sun and the rain

(59)
Two perfect daisies
Peered through rotted slats.
Thrive unattended

(60)
What law made these leaves
Form a platform canopy?
Nature's blase joke

26

(61)
The crawling bug
Made it up the balcony rail
To be flicked off

(62)
A whole other scene,
Slanted sunlight opens to
Days passing shade

(63)
Silhouettes, the last shadows
Before the moon is brighter
Than the setting sun

(64)
Synonymous sound-drop,
Traffic over a bridge and
Water under

(65)
Hoots beckon the eve.
How often did I have to learn
T'was the mourning dove

(66)
Stark dead white tree.
Dark moist dirt full of life
Both have and will give

(67)
Silence sits in peace
Listening to the wind
Sitting with a friend

(68)
Fluttering wings trill
Two birds emerge, one not quite
Following the other

(69)
Pause and ask the apps
To tell me what I hear and see
Goldfinches today

(70)
Approaching the trail
Yet no flies have stained
Your windshield

(71)
Morning after storm
Fallen branches line pathways
Here, cleared before noon

(72)
Suburban sunsets,
A trick with such beautiful light
Should keep driving West

(73)
Nature's neon contrasts
Trimmed trees line tele-routes
Red maples and yellow oaks

(74)
Cool easterly breeze
Compliments afternoon sun
As shadows lengthen

(75)
After birds and bees—
Petals, finished, curl under
Resigned to weather

(76)
The wind blew late
On an unbearable day
And a wish flew by

(77)
I pause to be filled
The cypress knees weren't meant for me
I respectfully leave

(78)
Time encapsulated—
Some flowers pressed in a notebook
Never seen again

(79)
Pond stagnant and green
Adjacent to stream, so screams
"Make it murky!"

(80)
Lurks behind a smile
Seen as if from a distance
Spring's last tree to bloom

(81)
Latched to sweetgum seeds
Suburban nostalgia pains
A burred memory

(82)
Lazy sun tamed giant,
A sweetgum by the sidewalk
Beware what falls

(83)
Privileged to
Sense the snake in your garden.
Only prey has learned

(84)
Crouched to take a photo
Right over a hornet's nest
Should have known better

(85)
Summer rain came through
The slats of boards we call home
Warmth still permeates

(86)
Humidity weighs
Malodorous. Even when
Searching for Zen

(87)
Wind's relief—only trend
The buzzing you can pretend
It doesn't follow

(88)
Summer, a death—still—
Dulls, Rankles, maybe shrivels.
Dying violets stain

(89)
The humidity
Hinders my attempt to think
About what to write

(90)
A time when perceptions lie
The sun between Earth and sky
"Hell is real"

Furlough Observations

(91)
Pull your children close
Pandemic after winter
Its own cold blanket

(92)
More days of sunshine
More days of cold, snow and rain
Out of office to see

(93)
Memorizing Blake's "Spring,"
Pacing the backyard, quarantined.
The neighbor applauds

(94)
Took up yo-yoing.
Able to remember how
To go around the world

(95)
Walk the same path for
40 days and 40 nights
Always something new seen

(96)
I can't see the line,
I know the reflected light
Hits just inside—Blurred

(97)
Harmonic reprieve,
Right above where the shade falls
Nothing. But look East

(98)
Lazy strut to day's end.
Right above where the shade falls
Nothing. But look West

(99)
I miss the cadence.
Too wary, meticulous.
So forced, zombie-like

(100)
Windmills along the state line
Spin by day
Flash red at night

(101)
Words said en francais
Describing features perceived
Only seems truthful

(102)
The best forgotten
Memory of
A splash in the pond

(103)
I miss the quiet
Freedom to leave and return.
Six stuck in a room

(104)
I beg don't touch me
To the people I want most
Love's selfish language

(105)
Steam alludes to heat
Communion to nourishment
Eats toast in silence

(106)
Consume the moment
To feed the craving of want
Unsatiated

(107)
Too alone to be
Or
Too surrounded to breathe

(108)
I form this no-one.
Eyes see this human shape with
Eyes vacant/hidden

(109)
Voices buzzing
Sweet prelude
To a thunderous show

(110)
Endorphin freedom:
Pace set, muscles fire, breathe hard
You only need overcome

(111)
Can you tell that I
Am subscribed to Dictionary's
Word of the Day?

(112)
In repetition
Beyond fractals origin
A revolving stage

(113)
Genius in repeat
"I know it's for the better"
Each brings new meaning

(114)
Peer down precipice
Erosion vs. my kick
Still two sides of chance

(115)
The first line
Could very well be
The last

(116)
Zyn Zen
Replace, but
Don't benefit

(117)
Why a snake?
The worm doesn't need
Its head

(118)
Streets with no sidewalks
Cars begrudgingly stay left
You're just walking home

(119)
Window rain droplets,
Crossed, tired eyes see
Gray mountain ranges

(120)
Truth now a scar
Evidence of my
"Endearing naivete"

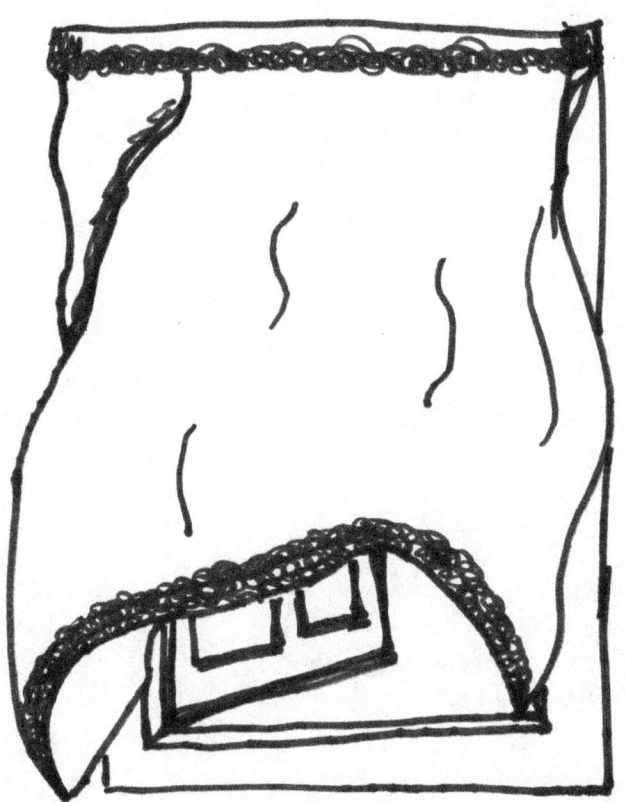

(121)
Early morning mist
A feeling not felt
Still a thought in your head

(122)
Often listening,
I turn into a
Bobblehead

(123)
I met you three times
It would terrify you to know
How patient I am

(124)
My thoughts spread like
Too many favorite songs
In different playlists

(125)
Traffic by the beach
Heads turn to catch a glance. A
Tomorrow assured

(126)
Where are we now?
In different cars, dancing
To the same music

(127)
Ride down Lake shore path
Cerulean lake reflects
Soltuid

(128)
I wanted to share
Rovelli's words, but
You should just read them

(129)
Across from the tents
Unloading onto Bittersweet
Busses passed by

(130)
Sitting in the yard
Wondering if I can indulge
And work today

(131)
Sunday afternoon
Alcoholic entropy
Frozen margaritas

(132)
It's not too late.
Really.
I just made up my mind

(133)
Thought Columbus
Might survive apocalypse
But the people won't

(134)
Saw my reflection
At the bottom of my
Coffee mug

(135)
Change in S is life.
As soon as I understand
I must start again

(136)
Billboard spit,
"Three nails fixed everything"
Blind turn ahead

(137)
Productive mornings
Don't end me waiting for
My old life at night

(138)
The cat's indignant,
My shared food placed on the floor.
"Do you need a plate?"

(139)
Occasionally
Go down Wareham Dr
To see a lovely door

(140)
Books I note to read
Never will reach
The top of my list

(141)
Breaking a habit
So I spent the night writing
Funny epitaphs

(142)
Father hands the hose
To his son throwing a fit,
So sprayed and laughed at

(143)
Playlist on, zoned out—
Reverie interrupted,
Trimming blade whirring

(144)
Adult Vacation:
Spend money, watch the sunset.
Happiest alone

(145)
Close your eyes.
Flashes stain your retina
Fast fading memory

(146)
Dare I tremble?
Reveal my excitement?
Vulnerable in want

(147)
Granularity
Change in configuration
A deck of cards shuffled

(148)
Try meditation.
Distracted by cricket song
Enlightened beat

(149)
Spontaneous act
When reading Jack Kerouac
Write down a haiku

(150)
You finally reach
The chemtrail lines you saw
A state away

(151)
Driving home from work—
Swear there were purple flowers
When I passed this morn'

(152)
Feign acceptance;
You may feel calm and peaceful
Left at the roadside

(153)
The Pacer is calm
When movement is unhindered
'Til the floor drops out

(154)
Foggy brain days pass
Like storm clouds that don't pour out
Anything useful

(155)
Nights I was a fool
In self-preservation
I forgot

(156)
When forward is down
Be aware that you can't fall
If your feet lead you

(157)
Sad that I have stopped
Rereading.
But there's just too much

(158)
A vulnerable sport
Learning is. Identify—
Bird song, the tune's name

(159)
Fresh and hopeful
Giving time to the morning
Rather, just attend

(160)
Enclosing feeling—
Mindful of wind through leg hairs
Supported body

(161)
There's an innocence
To knowing the melody
But not the words

(162)
Hubris of naming
Then disregarding meaning
Don't tell me a story

(163)
Metaphors the physics
Of the minds ability to spin
Over more than one axis

(164)
Time seems too filled;
Even relaxation now a slot
On a planner page

(165)
A giant pit in my stomach
To know better the history
To your popular story

(166)
History is always
Opposite popular culture
Fads too powerful

(167)
I've been practicing
Feeling detached, I tell myself.
Love is like belief

(168)
Zealous argument
Is the best reassurance
When in denial

(169)
Remember the smiles
Even if the joke does fade—
Discarded orange peels

(170)
I worry too much
Passing by careless eyes
That my shoes do squeak

(171)
History in ruins
Faded frescoes don't tell
Anything you'd get

(172)
Drama in the park
Geese flying overhead
Honks oblivious

(173)
Feel the wind's push
Arms extended out at side
Being here, flying

(174)
Deer no longer fear,
Yet have not learned how to
Cross the road

(175)
A vine hangs down
Bereft and useless, swinging
Few feet out of reach

(176)
Whisps intersect trails
Paths roll under roadways
Streams set to the side

Furlough Daydreams

(177)
Into your eyes placed
My obsessions phased like taste
Until I find out

(178)
Dear Emilia,
What a beacon you seemed.
Still, the fog of time

(179)
Alone, I think of you:
The freckle on your shoulder
Unknown on your back

(180)
I turned off the light
Didn't want to see you leave
The hallway silent

(181)
The Lucky Strikes
Were your father's.
Maybe you didn't notice

(182)
One day you quit.
A never dealt with projection
Can still abandon

(183)
Blissed out in torture.
It's not always like this
But today it is

(184)
Delirious
On a different existential plane
On a trip

(185)
I'm not sure
I let my hand slip
On the turn

(186)
A dream: Muse blown in
By zeitgeist. Calm yet wild
Eyes reverberate

(187)
The shadow of the tree,
Breeze that blows soft and warm. Always
I, Gallant Galwain

(188)
Moving in darkness
Lights blink in the night
Random seems magic

(189)
Was progress thwarted?
Seeing the daytime moon
I read up the page

(190)
Sometimes I lay down,
Feel tremors shake the ground,
Sense the world spinning round

(191)
Daydreaming, when
Grounded to reality—
Your foot tapping time

(192)
I challenge you
To break the moment
Or lean in

(193)
In the unlit field
The dead play in back of
Everyone's highs

(194)
I dream of old rooms,
Quarantined on parents' couch
Fantasized dreams dreamt

(195)
Riverbed resting
Fear laps at a soothing pace
Water snakes nearby

(196)
My dreams are
Semi-autofantastical
Obvious yearning

(197)
Listen with me
I'll be your novelty
You my projection

(198)
The wind blew late
On an unbearable day
And a wish flew by

(199)
Saying goodbye
I'll ask her to send me
The jacarandas

(200)
I attempt a sketch
Wishing I had queer
Eyes

(201)
New eyes—
Dream of driving you round
Singing while you sleep

(202)
In an open palm
Loved mutations can flourish
Ambiguous angels

(203)
Nothing that is new
Except colors, shades and mood
Listening to tunes

*Other Poems**

12/01/2020

Possibly heated sidewalks,
Free of the not so fresh snow,
My uninsured path is clear as
I steer in circles ever expanding.
Though never too far from
My doorstep, still icy in the shade,
I don't take the time to shovel.

60 in a 45

She caught my eye
Arm extending out the side
Window, I smiled
And may have sped by
Just to take a peek inside.

This took thinking of how you would take my
repost,
Or really, riposte,
A game I take seriously.
Points kept in eye contact.
My lips tug left to smirk
And you hooked to the line…

In times of isolation,
Fantasies expand and collide.
Too unoccupied to respect articulation
And separate true desire from momentary
Infatuation.

Myth transposing, cultural appropriation
(Thrill of the sneak, kiss in the shadows,
Cig out the window)

Put it all back where you found it.
I told your son the story of La Loba and
It was wrong and good and he loved it.
Out nonsense flows and it seems true
But I would never let You read it because
You would only say, "It's so good!"

She let you love her for frivolous reasons.
Learned the sounds
but still can't read those French lips,
I still won using your beliefs to change your mind
With egocentric comprehension
To humiliate my ego.

Aisle Seats

Our feet, opposite, reached into the aisle.
Soft colors—peripheral gluttony.
Feeling as if you stole a glance, as I.
Isn't animal magnetism funny?
I let my shawl drop from my shoulder
With no doubt you noticed my subtle show.
Reading, my stage, for when you looked over,
I imagined reality o'rthrown.
All the while you sleep. Your head tilts to face
Some possible dream, my musing a truth.
Repetitive movements to the same space.
And for that, I know I'll never get proof.
I suffered the courage to turn and view
Only to realize I envisioned You.

Angel Lake

Accents the horizon, blue shade of distance.
Land and sky contrast over expanse seen.
I feel full of some noisy silence,
For a purpose I have to believe.
Whether rage or joy, I cannot speak to,
Know only that it cannot be held in
And it comes with an irrational urge to
Extend and move, to reach each recess in
Sight, through shadows in trees to sunned peaks.
The feathered grass softly caress my shin,
An itch to serve as memory for weeks.
But I am still and silent, just breathing in.
I see me running across the valley
As I imagine the eagle flies, Free.

Haikus to Irish Tunes

I Don't Change to Change for You

Incomplete and genuine
She turned to me and said, "Honey,
What did you do that for?"

Never heard those words before
I was sure, such a curse never lighted
My door.

I smiled, frozen, and turned round
Couldn't see her way up or which way down
Into the deep brown of the bar.

She took my hand, a tug-remand,
A sweetgum-burr
This wasted holy land.

I do it again.

Linger here, have a beer
Karaoke, cracker dear?
Oh, don't be so insincere.
This taunt, I don't hear.

Erin Flanagan

Incomplete and genuine
She turned to me and she said, "Honey,
What did you do that for?"

I frown, relieved for what I don't see.
My image not her reality,
Projections only mine.

I follow Broadway North
My quartz heart fixed on a freckle
A night's worth.

I spent some money and forgot her name
But her question still remained
A flower in my brain.

Priviledged Wounds Fester

Praying that your prayers work.
That self-gratifying feeling of offering to help
When you know you cannot—
Realized in the shock when they demand
Your presence NOW.

I, separate and unanswering,
While they become frantic,
Watch as if nothing were happening;
And my good humor grows.
Possibly taking life from what is lost.

The day plays and the hectic concern tapers.
I look forward to seeing you smile at me.
The time comes, and you change your plans.
Ash falls and the present becomes history.

Random Composed

When I turned 28, I asked,
"What's the difference between a Buddist
And a psychopath?"

Cleverly modified idioms,
Atheistic materialism,
Why wouldn't they stress the phonetics in transla-
tion?
I filled in only my own context.

My roots are surprising
But I cannot stake any claim by them.

Visions in paranoia
Bass buzzing like a notification.
Memories of sound,
The scene posed for me.

A man comes every night to tell his son
Mostly truths and usually throws in a lie,
The lie did not stand out amongst the truths—
Thus there was no concept of a lie.

Haikus to Irish Tunes

Don't we mostly just check out ass
Gazing out the bus window?

Each variation, it's own unique variable.

There will be a time in your life that politics seem to
matter,
That the world seems to be on the brink of change,
That the plot seems menacing and layered,
That the players seem "different"
That their message is genuine.

I stopped using social media
So I'm mixing up my holidays:
Came out on International Women's Day,
Went to Poet's church on Easter,
And sang that New Years song on your birthday.

Before she slammed the door
She shouted back,
"Your Orchid looks fake because you spent
18 months speaking love to it every day."

Due to whatever justification is needed
The moment it could be relevant.
Retroactive excuses.

I'm so scared to look up,
Not due to experience,
So often relieved by kind eyes.

She told me, "I've been thinking 'bout the little
things"
Behind her smile, hope of a future.

She tilts to the left
I feign words for her neck
That the Irish have said could look just like a
swan's.
Her hair, it was gold,
So I know, I only like what I know.

When I was in her arms, she laughed like a god.
Who do you tell your fantasies to?
Only the ones who experience it with you.

I let time slide
By
Formula a manipulation to see pattern.
I got high
And hypnotized myself—

Quit smoking the next day.

My soul, attached to my thoughts,
Chemical and electrical reactions.
And to think I could be immortal
without the physical…
Ha

I am blessed because I decided to love ambiguity
Kahneman states, "System one does not keep track
of what alternates it rejects."

To The Tune of Carrickfergus

I dreamt I was out in Chicago
Just like those nights we went bar to bar.
Through hazy heated and windy grasses
That smiling face, always turned from me.

But the crowd is wide and I have social anxiety
Though I still wish I had wings to fly
To you and say that I love you
And that smile would then turn to me.

My barroom days bring back sad reflections
Of trying to punch through my own repression.
My barroom friends and my loving strangers
I've let pass on now to only memory.

Then I'd spend my days in endless roving
Forgetting time and consequence
To live only in those moments
Watching That smile from across the bar.

Ah, but in Columbus, it is reported
On Instagram pages still every day
That brutal combination of atmosphere and choice,

Still I'll sing today and miss the clink.

I'm free today and I'm fairly sober
A gallant gal walking through the town.
Ah, But I see you 'round every corner
I believe I only wish to wave you by.

Untitled

Where is my mind?

I feel ok
I feel distracted
I feel like I have forgotten everything
I feel like it's more of the same thing
I feel content
I feel anxiety prowling the edges of my mind
I feel capable
I can't feel a thing
I am marked by idiocy
I am stated to now
Not before
I was clear
This is nonsense
I am lounging
This page is slanted.

She touched my arm and held my hand
But she wasn't playing the game with me.

I was happy when Paul with the sad eyes
And Christine, the queen

Derailed my untrusting attention.
They saw something lovely—
But the mark they looked past was the truth,
And my kind eyes, only an enabling refuge.

I should get Tattooed
"All my words come back to me in shades of medi-
ocrity."

Grounding truths
Scars inflicted on the body
Why is truth scarring?
Why is beauty unscathed?
Maybe innocence is only the lack before
Experiences make true the cliches.

Shall I jot down some references
To heighten my genius?
I'll use Aristotle's name to present
What 'I' understood he meant.

How many translations have turned more
Of the same thoughts to power and belief
Allowing the diminishment of
Future thought? Limiting
Only if you then feel you don't need to.
But a mountain to

Stand upon if willing to
Glance into the expanse.

So then, I thank you,
Aristotle, even though I
Do not remember anything
I have read by you in this instant.
It's the thought—Nay, the intention—that matters.

I'm full of emptiness
Please come squash it
With your touch.
I'll accept even just handholding.
Tether me to reality
Make me more than my rationale
"Smile and everything will be alright."

Phoebe, is that you?

Attribute incorrectly,
Still a tribute.

For it was Alice Phoebe Lou.

Nonsense, a jitter twitter
Wanting pating
Wanting wanting

For your lips approach
I will probably balk.

I may look like I'm waiting
But I need this time too.
Don't feel bad, I will move
On without communicating
When I need to.
Then, you can feel bad.

Erin Flanagan

Watching My Brothers

I choose to live in a world of tension,
Perpetuated by hesitation,
Waiting for Fate
To nod and open the gate.

They live their lives within smoke-filled rooms,
Hazy security, their forever groom.
Not assuming they pose for photographs
Already taken before they learned to laugh.

The beat picks up to heighten an atmosphere:
Time situates an I against them.
But I forgot it's at a past I peer
Where I stood amidst, and still saw within·

Haikus to Irish Tunes

Erin Flanagan

**If you enjoyed this collection of poems & haikus,
please take a moment to leave a review.*

Disclaimer:

Not all of the songs in the "To reek or not to reek-for you" playlist are Irish. Some are Celtic as well.

To reek or not to reek-for you playlist

HIYA - Ross Ainsie and Jarlath Henderson

HEADLIFTER - Project Smok

BIG SKY - Bene & Cormac

CHERRY BLOSSOM - Fourth Moon

TWO TREES / TONY - Brian Finnegan

HUY HUY! - Hamish Napier

HYPERSOMNIA - Ali Levack

GORDON'S - Gnoss

ELLIE GOES WEST - Flook

FARE THEE WELL, NORTHUMBERLAND... - The Cottars, & etc.

THE WIND THAT SHAKES THE BARLEY - Solas

AIR FÀIR AN LÀ - Niteworks, Sian

LEAVING UIST / LOCHABER... - Michael MacGoldrick, & etc.

THE TORTOISE AND THE HAIR - Flook

FORWARD THINKING - Assynt

HORÒ GUN TOGAINN AIR HÙGAN FHATHAST THU - Staran

PROMISE - Project Smok

Illustration Credits

40-42: "Trees and Flowers" by Megan Flanagan

49-51: "First Tree" by Megan Flanagan

58-60: "Flowers" by Megan Flanagan

61-63: "Group of Trees" by Megan Flanagan

118-120: "Window" by Kelly Flanagan

124-126: "Moon" by Megan Flanagan

133-135: "Chair" by Evan Hansen

189-191: "Abstract" by Evan Hansen

198-200: "Dandelion" by Evan Hansen

Notes

(13) Hamish Napier, a Musician in Glasgow, wrote the phrase "Vivid sonic images" to describe his music in his album leaflet for *The River*. Napier played with Jarlath Henderson during a United States tour, and as I was waiting to see them at the Irish American Heritage Center in Chicago, I was drinking a pint of Magners at the bar and reading through the little album book. I was blown away by the pure and simple truth to this qualifier.

(25) The Clancy Brothers are a famed Irish/Irish-American group performing mostly in the 60s and 70s. They were part of the large folk music trend and brought many Irish drinking and rebel tunes to popularity. My reference to the Clancy Brothers is personal. I listened to them almost exclusively for the most formative years of my life, pretty much until I became a teenager who realized I was supposed to try and fit in.

(79) This Haiku is in reference to a classic scene of jealousy from the opera *Tosca*. The line, "Make it murky," is not in the opera—to paraphrase it's more like 'make her eyes brown.'

(87) I was reading *Plain Bad Heroines* by Emily M. Danforth when I wrote this Haiku.

(102) This Haiku is in reference to a conversation two Zen monks were once recorded to have had, Basho and

Buccho. Basho wrote many Haikus and I have brought him in to reveal some inspiration and give thanks.

(113) While a popular phrase, "I know it's for the better." In this Haiku, it specifically references Phoebe Bridger's song *Waiting Room*.

(124) I made up the word "soltuid." I was obsessed with the awareness of light following your line of vision over a reflective surface and I wanted to make it a single thought or word. This one stuck with me.

(125) Carlo Rovelli is a physicist and author. His book, *The Order of Time*, is one that maybe changed my outlook of the world, or opened my eyes. If you can't tell from my Haikus, I reference my understanding of entropy often and this book helped solidify that.

(156) This Haiku references Jack Kerouac's *The Dharma Bums*.

(169) Discarded orange peels are in reference to JD Salinger's short story *Teddy*.

"To The Tune of Carrickfergus" is a poem and song I wrote off the song *Carrickfergus*, which is an old Irish folk song—and I probably ruined it.

In "Random Composed," I reference Daniel Kahneman's *Thinking Fast and Slow.*

In "Untitled," I quote "All my words come Back to me in shades of mediocrity" from Simon and Garfunkel's song *Homeward Bound*. I also quote "Smile and everything will be alright" from Alice Phoebe Lou's song *Dusk*.

Acknowledgments

I would like to thank my siblings, Johnny, Kelly, David, Tommy, Megan, Nathan, and Matthew. You all are my heart.

Kelly and Megan were contributors with a few of their wonderful sketches, and Megan also is the illustrator of the cover of *Haikus to Irish Tunes*.

My brother Tommy is my sounding board and almost everything I write is seen by his eyes before anyone else's. Tommy Flanagan is also a musician, and you should check out his album *Teapot* on whatever streaming service you use.

I also must thank the Hansen brothers, Evan and Rob. Evan created some awesome sketches for this book, and these are the most supportive and artistic guys to have at your back.

I am also so thankful for my editor, Flor Ana Mireles, and my publisher, Indie Earth Publishing, for giving me a chance and being so positive and supportive.

I want to give one last big thank you to the ML "Red" Trabue Nature Reserve where I have spent hundreds of hours walking and finding peace and writing since the beginning of quarantine.

About the Author

© Photography by Evan Hansen

Erin Flanagan is a writer who lives in Columbus, Ohio and is possibly an orange peel. She spends too much time reading and loves hours-long walks in any park, listening to the birds over headphones. *Haikus to Irish Tunes* is her literary debut.

Connect with Erin on Instagram:
@erinflanagan2552

About the Publisher

INDIE EARTH
PUBLISHING

Indie Earth Publishing Inc. is an independent, author-first co-publishing company based in Miami, FL, dedicated to giving writers the creative freedom they deserve when publishing their poetry, fiction, and short story collections. Indie Earth provides its authors a plethora of services meant to aid them in their book publishing experiences and finally feel they are releasing the book of their dreams.

With Indie Earth Publishing, you are more than just an author, you are part of the Indie Earth creative family, making a difference one book at a time.

www.indieearthbooks.com

For inquiries, please email:
indieearthpublishinghouse@gmail.com

Instagram: @indieearthbooks